PATTY SUERS

HOW WE LOVE

The Ultimate Guide on Learning How to Love Unconditionally, Learn The Secrets To Removing Attachments and Loving With No Conditions

Descrierea CIP a Bibliotecii Naționale a României
PATTY SUERS
   HOW WE LOVE. The Ultimate Guide on Learning How to Love Unconditionally, Learn The Secrets To Removing Attachments and Loving With No Conditions / Patty Suers. – Bucharest: Editura My Ebook, 2020
   ISBN 978-606-983-588-3

PATTY SUERS

HOW WE LOVE

The Ultimate Guide on Learning How to Love Unconditionally, Learn The Secrets To Removing Attachments and Loving With No Conditions

My Ebook Publishing House
Bucharest, 2020

TABLE OF CONTENTS

FOREWORD

The greatest power that mankind could ever achieve is the power of unconditional love. This is when people love with no limitations, conditions or boundaries. This type of love is also comparable to true love which is used to describe love between lovers. But unconditional love is mostly used to describe the love for family members and other highly committed relationships. This book will tell you everything about giving and receiving unconditional love. Get all the info you need here.

Unconditional Love

Steps On Removing Attachments and To Love
Unconditionally

CHAPTER 1

INTRODUCTION

Synopsis

Most of the time, people mistook true love from unconditional love. When they meet the partners that they really want to spend the rest of their life with, they would always say that their love for them is unconditional, but after a few trials in the relationship, they would go separate ways and hate each other.

This is not what unconditional love means because when you say unconditional love, this is like a "Mother's Love" – a love for her children that never fades no matter what trials or problems may come their way.

The Basics

Unconditional love knows no boundaries, no limitations and no conditions. When you love someone unconditionally, you are just there to support, love, protect and care for them without asking for anything in return.

The love for your family members is truly an unconditional love because no matter what happens, you will always stay as a family that loves and support each other even if you are all separated and have your own family.

A perfect example for an unconditional love is the parents' love for their child. Whatever problems come their way – their test score, an argument, a strong belief and life changing decisions they make, still, the love between them stays unconditional and unchanging.

Loving a friend can also be considered as unconditional love if you love them without asking for anything or something in return.

It is hard to give your unconditional love to someone that is not related to you by blood because with just one mistake, the trust will be gone and it is hard to love if you don't trust that person.

CHAPTER 2

NATURE OF AN UNCONDITIONAL LOVE

Synopsis

Almost everyone wants to love and be loved unconditionally with no limitations, bounds, hesitations or conditions. You want love that is not just given by your family but a love that could be a part of your own family. It is hard to give unconditional love if you cannot love your own self. In order for you to give unconditional love, you should always start by loving yourself. If you are burdened by so many distress or you have so many difficulties in life, you will surely find it hard to love unconditionally.

What's The Nature

You are the only one who can help yourself face all your difficulties in life. You can overcome the limitations of your life if you have the will to do so. Love is just there and is limitless only if you can see it through your will. But once you are trapped in your past, you will never see the goodness in love and you will surely find it hard to give your love to someone.

This will be available anytime if you turn your attention to it and use its amazing potential to free yourself from your limitations. This also requires intent and practice to allow the energy to fully permeate your daily experience.

If you want to know what true love is, then you should start loving yourself. By loving yourself, this will also allow you to love other people and share it to anyone or anything around you.

You should first consider determining your feelings towards yourself mentally, physically, spiritually and emotionally.

When clearing your mind, you also need to walk out in your shell and view the beauty of the world. This will keep you energized and will give you strength to face your journey. With a clear and positive mind, you'll have the power to manifest anything. All you need to do is believe that you can do it.

CHAPTER 3

HOW TO REMOVE ATTACHMENTS IN YOUR LOVE LIFE

Synopsis

If you are attached to your love life so much, you will end up suffering in the end. Being attached to someone or something so deeply is also bad for you because the moment that it's gone, you will find it hard to move and face the reality. When you are attached to someone, it also means that you are devoted to that person and you cannot live without them. Once they are gone or out of your control, you will feel the burden of distress and you will find it hard to move on.

What Happens

This is why there are so many people who are losing control of their life because of love life or too much depression. You have to learn how to remove the attachments in your love life if you want to find unconditional love. Removing all the attachments will also free you from sufferings and burdens.

If you will learn how to love unconditionally, then you will also learn how to free yourself from your limits and be able to express yourself freely.

Getting in a relationship takes a lot of courage because you will know that as your relationship gets deeper, you will also encounter several trials that you need to face. These trials will make you and your relationship stronger because of the lessons that you will learn from them. But you should never let yourself be attached to these mistakes because they will only pull you down and lower your self-esteem.

How to remove the attachments in your love life will start from yourself. By taking full control of your feelings and knowing your limits, you will be able to adjust easily in your situation. It is also important that you have an open mind, so that you can think of all the positive things and come to your senses.

Sometimes, when you are so attached to your partner, you forget about other things that make you happy. Your world only revolves around that one person and when he or she leaves you, it feels like your world has fallen apart. This is a negative feeling that you should avoid and that is why you should try to remove the attachments you have in your love life. Always consider going out on your own and doing what you love when you are alone or what makes you happy.

CHAPTER 4

LEARNING HOW TO LOVE UNCONDITIONALLY

Synopsis

Learning how to love unconditionally means freeing yourself from so much distress and accepting yourself more than anything else in this world. You can only learn to love yourself if you can admit to yourself that you are worthy to love and be loved. Unconditional love is given most of the time to your family members or loved ones. This is because a family always stays together no matter what happens and you are not just related by names but also by blood, so no one can ever take that away from you.

What Is It

But when you are physically attached to someone and you learn to love them, this is what you call conditional love. Love is different if you will show it differently to other people. This is why it is even harder to know if what you feel is really love or not. If you want to love unconditionally, then you will have to let go of all your doubts and start accepting yourself. Learn how to forgive and forget all things that you have done so that you can better show some love to people without asking for something in return because you already have what you want.

By loving other people and accepting their differences and true attitude, you will also learn how to love unconditionally.

Conditional love is given with certain limits and conditions. You only love because they made you happy and they can fill in all the emptiness in you. As your love gets deeper, you can start your own family and this is when your unconditional love begins. Once you have your own family together, you can give and experience unconditional love.

If you will define love, you can have different meanings to it but when you try to give unconditional love, you will find it hard to show it. If you only love a person because you wanted something in return, then this is truly a conditional love.

CHAPTER 5

BASIC STEPS IN MAKING YOUR LOVE LIFE COUNT

Synopsis

If you are in a relationship and you want to improve your love life, then you should learn the basic steps in making your love life count. Knowing the important steps to make your love life count will also help you have a successful life. As you go on with your life, you will encounter trials along the way and if you will not be able to handle them properly, your relationship will surely suffer and fall apart in the long run. Sometimes, it takes to love again especially if you had been in a serious relationship and you broke up.

It even hurts to see that your ex-partner is now happy with someone else. But this is a fact that people need to understand. Life should always go on no matter what pains you have to go through. Love is magical and you need to believe that everything happens for a reason. So if your relationship didn't work, for sure, someone better is about to come into your life.

To help you better understand everything, here are some of the steps that you need to follow so that you can have a successful love life.

The Steps

Love Yourself

Almost 70% of relationships end up in break up. The main reason for this is that people are so attached to their partners that they tend to forget they also have their needs. They are so busy doing something for their partners to make them happy that they forget about their own happiness.

If you love your partner more than you love yourself, then surely, your love life will not work out. If you really want to be happy, then you also need to do the things that will make you happy. Do not just focus on making other people happy.

Acceptance

Acceptance is also important in a relationship because it is what makes your relationship stronger. One fault is not enough reason to break up because if you know how to accept their sorry or accept your mistake, then you will still have time to catch up together.

Also, you need to remember that your partner is not perfect, so as you. You should learn to accept the difficulties and the downsides of the person you love, so that you can be happy with each other.

Forgive and Forget

When you say you forgive a person, it means that you should also forget what happened. You have to do this so that every time you have a misunderstanding, you will not go back to the past and argue for the same issue.

If you will learn how to forgive and forget, then you will also learn to accept the situation and you can move on without any regrets. It is really hard to forget the past but it is also important that you learn to forget so that you will not be carrying the burden in your heart for a long time.

Make sure that when you forgive, it is really sincere and you accept it, so that you can easily move on and make healing process easier for both of you.

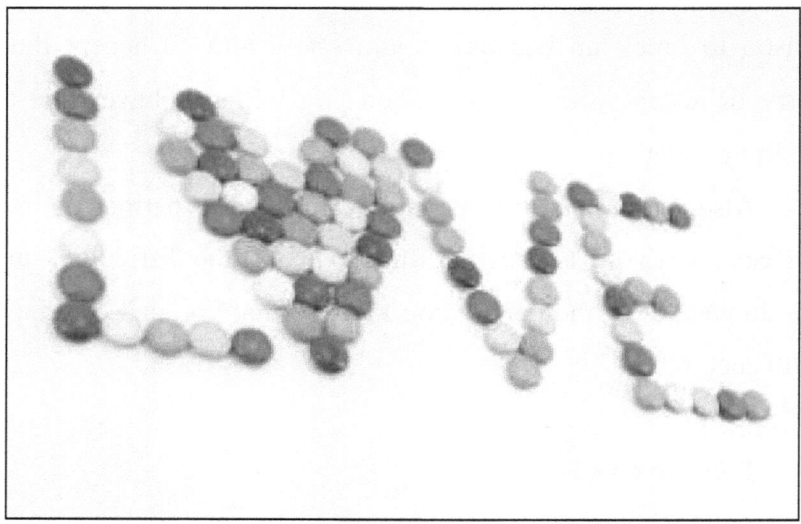

CHAPTER 6

THE A-Z OF LOVE LIFE

Synopsis

There are so many things that you need to consider if you want to have a happy and long love life. The A-Z of love life should be considered as your guidelines so that you will know the best things to do to strengthen your relationship. You don't need to be perfect in a relationship since nobody is perfect; and surely, you will make mistakes at some point in your relationship.

What you need is a simple guideline that will help you face several changes and trials in your relationship. It is like a step by step guideline that you need to follow so that you can have a good direction in your love life.

A-Z

In some research, you will find the different meanings of A-Z of love life. For example, A stands for attention, which means that you need to put proper attention in your relationship.

Taking your relationship for granted is not a good idea because you also need to consider the feelings of your partner. Once you are committed to someone, it also mean that you need to give them enough time and attention.

The letter X stands for EX, which means your past. Once a person is considered as your ex, then there is no more point in going back. You need to move on with your new love.

You cannot stay harboring feelings for your ex because it will only cause you more pain and you will only prolong your agony.

The A-Z of love life has different meanings that you need to learn, but one thing is for sure. Whatever their meaning is, it should always come first in your priority if you want to have a happy love life.

CHAPTER 7

TAPPING INTO THE UNLIMITED POWER
OF THE UNIVERSE

Synopsis

Receiving unconditional love is a great feeling that everyone wants to experience. Of course, you get unconditional love from your parents because it is already given. You can also have unconditional love from someone that you love if you also deserve to be loved. Every person wants to experience unconditional love especially from their parents because this is what makes or creates a person.

Some people are afraid to show their unconditional love because they never experienced it from their parents. If you are one of the kids who did not experience unconditional love because of your ugly past, it doesn't mean that you should also be a bad parent to your kids.

You already know how it feels, so there is no point in taking away from your kids what was already taken away from you and that is unconditional love.

Here are 10 reasons why you need to have unconditional love.

1. **Accept your imperfection and forgive yourself.** Unconditional love means being true to one's self. If you can accept your imperfections, then surely, you can give unconditional love to other people. There is no such thing as a perfect human and what you are up to is not just being a good person, but receiving love itself. Every child needs full attention, presence, care, affection and appreciation from their parents, not perfection. Don't be afraid to make mistakes. As long as you know how to forgive yourself, you can find a way to correct your mistakes. You can start by changing the way you talk about yourself. When you hear negative thoughts about you, always remind yourself that your goal is not perfection but to love yourself and other people.

2. **Just like a muscle, unconditional love also needs workout.** Almost everyone is carrying a heavy lift in their life such as lies, mistakes, pretence and other difficulties. If you will always carry this load in your life, then you will end up fainting

and giving up. You need to start building your muscle by showing unconditional love to yourself and everyone around you. You can try to set all those worries away and build your muscle, so that you can fight against the heavy trials of life. Don't let your child see your sufferings because this will add an extra heavy baggage to your child's experience.

3. **Embrace yourself.** You know that if you are always connected with your inner fountain of life, it will overflow to your children and you will become a better parent that is more supportive, loving, caring, patient and more joyful. In order to love your children unconditionally, you always need to stay full so that you will never run out or become empty. Once you are stressed out or you are carrying a lot of burdens in your heart, you will never have the chance to give yourself unconditional love. You need to embrace yourself with love and acceptance because this can also be passed on to your family.

4. **Forgive your parents.** You should start forgiving your parents as they are human too. Nobody is perfect and people have their own imperfections. There are times that your parents will also forget about you and you will feel left out and abandoned. You just need to understand that they are not also

perfect and they have a different burden to keep; that is why they cannot provide the attention and love you want.

5. **Heal your life so that you can heal your soul**. According to love experts, the only way out is through your soul. If your heart is wounded, then surely, your soul is also suffering from pains. Some people believe that it is better to get hurt physically because you can easily see the scar and put medicine on it, but when you are hurt inside, it is hard to see how deep the wound is and it takes a long time to heal. If you want to experience unconditional love, then you should start healing your soul first. Be brave enough to face your mistakes and do the right things to make up for your mistakes. If you will continue to keep your burdens inside, then you will just waste your time trying to heal your soul. Once your soul is healed, you can now go on with your life happily and freely. Your anger will only cause you too much pain and sufferings.

6. **Accept your loved ones unconditionally**. Showing unconditional love is not enough if it is not accepted. You should learn to accept the facts first, so that you can love your child unconditionally. This also means that your child doesn't need to earn or prove something just for you to give them the love they need. Whatever your child comes out to be, you

should accept them because you are their parent and that is not made by choice but God's will. The moment you are born, you will immediately feel this unconditional love from your parents. As a parent, you should never take this for granted and you have to show your children and your family that kind of love.

7. **Show Up and Lighten Up**. If you have made mistakes as a parent, then you should join this club. It is not considered as a mistake if it is used for your child's future. There is no need to have a good answer in all of your decisions and there is no need to fix all situations. All you need to do is to love your child and forget about fears. Your child doesn't need all material things in the world, because all they need is acceptance and complete care.

8. **Take high road**. Taking the high road means that you are calm, patient and well responding to your child's needs. When you say low road, this is when you are stressed, resentful and exhausted. You are always angry, terrified and you lack patience most of the time. Always stay on the high road so that your child will always look up to you and respect you. You should avoid tantrums because this is what your child will see in you and it can be carried when they grow up and be parents.

Being in a high road will give you peace of mind and you will also feel so much love around you.

9. **Become a parent of love and not anger.** It is very easy to love unconditionally if you know how to set your goals. Being a parent is a lifetime task and responsibility that you should do properly and part of this is to love your child unconditionally. When you cannot love yourself, how can you love your child unconditionally?

Apart from yourself, it is your family that you should share your unconditional love with. You should always show them that you care for them as much as you care for yourself. Anger will not give you the right answers because it will only worsen your problem. Your child will never learn if you are always angry and shouting at them whenever they make mistakes.

10. **Practice makes perfect.** If you want to learn how to love unconditionally, you should practice every day. You should always try to reach out to your child when things get wrong and try to talk to them if you want them to change. There is no such thing as perfect parents and children. But you can surely give your unconditional love to your family if you want to. You can

start your practice every day by simply showing care and affection to your child. Never give up in showing your unconditional love to your family because as a parent, you will always need to try over and over again.

Being a family is different from your love life because you also give a different kind of love to each other. These 10 reasons are important to remember so that you will know why people need to have unconditional love. Everyone needs to feel that they are loved unconditionally and it starts in your family, so you must never stop loving your children so that they will grow up knowing that you love them unconditionally.

This way, there will be many people who can give their unconditional love to other persons too. It is not so difficult to give your love to someone especially if you are born in a family with so much love.

CHAPTER 8

HOW TO PROVE AN UNCONDITIONAL LOVE

Synopsis

If you want to show your unconditional love to your family, then you should start loving yourself. There is no such thing as proving that you can give unconditional love because you just need to show it.

If you cannot show them that you love yourself, then how can you give unconditional love to everyone? You can simply prove your unconditional love to everyone if you know how to deal with things accordingly, when you are patient, caring and you know how to forgive and forget.

Unconditional love is given to someone who also loves himself. For you to give unconditional love, you must love yourself as well. There is no certain proof when you give this kind of love because it can be felt naturally. People will see if they are receiving unconditional love because they can tell it right from the start.

How To

If you love unconditionally, you are willing to sacrifice everything for your loved ones. You are not asking for something in return because you love them more than anything else in the world.

No matter how hard things may be, you can patiently wait because your love is there. There are no limitations, no conditions and no boundaries in a mother's love. You always accept and love your children no matter what type of person they become.

As for the real unconditional love, you are willing to wait patiently for the right time when your child will also feel the same way towards you. Just like in a relationship of two people, you will know if it is really unconditional love if both of you are feeling the same towards each other.

There is no way you can prove your unconditional love because there is no exact word to describe it because you can only show it. If you feel that you have this unconditional love for someone, then it means that you are also ready to feel hurt and pain just to prove your love for this special person.

CHAPTER 9

HOW TO MAKE YOUR LOVE LIFE COUNT
FOR THE OTHER

Synopsis

It is hard to keep your love life going steady if both of you are not sincere in what you feel. It is very important that couples have an open communication with each other.

It is also necessary that they both accept each other for their own differences. In a relationship, it is normal that couples argue about someone or something. This is only a proof that people are not perfect and they have different ways of thinking about things. But the important thing is that at the end of the day, they still got each other.

Make It Count

If you love your partner unconditionally, then you should trust him or her more than anyone else. You should avoid thinking about things that will ruin your relationship; and if you are true to your partner, you will also never do crazy things that will take away their trust. Once that trust is broken, you will find it hard to be together again because whatever you do, there will always be doubts deep inside you.

If you want to experience unconditional love in your love life, then you should start by loving yourself. How can you give your love to someone if you don't even love or trust yourself? Both of you need to love unconditionally, so that you can have a successful love life. Being in a relationship means having a big responsibility because you not only think about yourself but also about your partner. Learning the basic steps in making your love life successful is important so that you can have a successful relationship.

You will always encounter trials and difficulties and that is normal because you are human and you are not perfect. You just need to stay strong in facing your mistakes and make sure that you know how to accept your wrongs. Sometimes, it hurts to love again especially if you had been in a serious relationship and you ended breaking up.

Wrapping Up

Killing Attachments in an Unconditional Love

Being so attached to your partner will only ruin your relationship. If you are so attached to each other, then you will find it hard to deal with other people without each other. The attachment is like being very dependent to something or someone. This is not a good idea because if you are separated, then you will find it hard to move on because you are very dependent to that person. You also need to have your own life even if you are together.

It is right that you give each other the right privacy that both of you need, so that both of you can have sometime alone. You need to kill or get rid of that attachment with your partner, so that both of you will have the best time in your relationship. You will enjoy each other more if you have no limits, no boundaries and no conditions in your relationship. This is what we call unconditional love. When you give unconditional love, you don't need to expect more, you don't need to ask for something in return and you are not so much attached to each other.

Always consider giving your relationship your own privacy because when you have privacy, it means that you trust each other. You are not afraid of giving space because you know that you both need this in order for your relationship to work and grow. Before you enter in a relationship, you need to make sure that you are ready and willing to take the risks that come with it. Loving is not always fun, happy and thrilling as it will also make you cry and feel hurt at some point. If there is open communication between the two of you, even if you are far from each other, you can be sure that you will always stay happy and in love no matter what happen.

Giving unconditional love is so important and it is also free. With this kind of love around, for sure, you will have the perfect partner in the world. You need someone that you can trust, rely on and share your life with until your die; and you can only find it when you learn to give your unconditional love.

Always remember that loving unconditionally also means that you love with all your heart and with no doubts, limits, boundaries or conditions.

9 786069 835883

Printed by Libri Plureos GmbH in Hamburg,
Germany